© David Beresford 2024
First edition February 2024

All rights reserved. No part of this book may be reproduced or distributed in any form without prior written permission from the author, with the exception of non-commercial uses permitted by copyright law

Contents

Forward	5
Before the beginning	7
Institutional life	21
Freedom at last	29
My first church	33
More of the same	45
Go North Young Man	54
You're not supposed to laugh	67
The Big Apple	70
A new start	76
No pain no gain	92
Fresh faces	98
The times they are a changing	105
By the seaside	108
Geoff and Jenny	116
And finally…	120

Confessions of a Pentecostal Pastor

Forward

For several years friends have been saying, David, you must write a book about the stories, and experiences that have happened to you, and the interesting people you have known in the Christian ministry.

Let me say first that most Christians that I have had the privilege of meeting, have been wonderful well-balanced individuals that have been a great influence and inspiration to me. I have also encountered others who, shall we say were a little different.

This book is about some of the more amusing and interesting character's that I have met, and the events that have happened to me. It is not an autobiography, but a few snapshots of the incidents and people that I hope you enjoy, and that may bring a smile to your face and encourage you to follow our Lord and Saviour Jesus Christ more joyfully.

Chapter 1

Before the beginning

We had recently moved from a little country cottage in the small Lancashire town of Westhoughton to the larger town of Blackburn, where my father had accepted the pastorate of the Elim Pentecostal Church there.

We brought with us our large tom cat which went by the not so imaginative name of Tom. I took him to the front door of our large, terraced house which was to be our future home, to give him a glimpse of his new surroundings. But no sooner had he cast his eye on the cobbled street and his nose smelt the sultry air polluted by smoke from the coal fired chimneys, than he jumped out of my arms ran across the road and disappeared into an alleyway. We looked everywhere for him and called him constantly, but we never saw him again. It was 1950 and I was six years old.

The manse which was our home, was situated near the town centre and it always seemed to be full of visitors. My mother never locked the front door in those days, so after the good Christian people of Blackburn had done their shopping, many of them just wandered into our living room, drank our tea, ate our food, and kept my parents talking for hours. My younger brother Philip, sister Ruth and I were shunted off to the parlour when some delicate or confidential matters were being discussed.

From time to time, however, something far more unsettling happened. Not only did they pass through... but they stayed - often for months on end! One lady we called aunty May stayed with us for two years recovering from nervous trouble. By the time she left I think we all had nervous trouble.

After returning to her home my father visited her and asked if she was feeling any better to which she replied yes, then, quick as a flash added, "Which is a sure sign that I'm going to get worse." I don't think optimism was her strong point.

Another interesting person was Ethel. Ethel was from Wigan. She had some physical complaint or other and stayed with us for several months. She would never admit that she was ill, saying only that she had the *symptoms* of an illness.

Admitting to an illness for Pentecostal people in the 1950s and 60s was tantamount to living in unbelief, and no card-carrying Pentecostal wanted *that* stigma hung around his or her neck. So many of them suffered in silence or lived in denial.

I remember that she had a set of ill-fitting false teeth which clicked like castanets each time she spoke. Mealtimes were a nightmare. The clicking and sucking she needed to retain dental equilibrium was more than I could stomach, and frequently put me off my food. She also played hymns for hours on our piano and had a rather unique style of delivery; the left hand hitting the keys slightly before the right hand. Thus, producing a sort of lunging effect to the music.

We had many visitors in those days. I well remember two missionaries turning up for the weekend. They had come to speak at our church, to tell us of the work they were doing in Africa, and to drum up financial support for their ministry. They also had bookings at other Elim churches in the area but for some reason they always returned to us after the meetings. I guess they must have liked the arrangement because they stayed with us for three months. My father said that he had to resort to prayer to get rid of them, as we were keeping them both for free and dad's salary was very small.

I well remember a middle-aged couple staying in our front room for a while. The husband didn't attend church, but his wife was a member at Zion, the local Assembly of God church. They had failed to keep up with the mortgage payments on their house and had been evicted. Why her own church couldn't help I'm not sure, but my parents took pity on them, and they stayed with us. Among the small number of personal items, they brought with them, was an old seventy-eight wind up record player. From morning to night, he would play songs from the forties and fifties. The oft repeated favourite was "I'll take you home again Kathleen" sung by Joseph Locke, the famous Irish tenor. I must have heard it hundreds of times and wondered whether Kathleen would ever be taken home again, as she seemed quite content with us, the couple stayed so long.

There must have been times when we were visitor free but as a child it seemed to me that people just came one after another. As I'm remembering some of them now, I think of Gustav, who would come occasionally, - we called him Guss; he was a travelling evangelist whose home was a converted ambulance. He would turn up out of the blue from time to time. His ambulance was fitted with loudspeakers so he could preach the gospel at fêtes, county shows, or any public space he could find. He also carried a large bundle of gospel tracts which he distributed to those who were interested in the gospel - and to those who weren't.

A lovely elderly couple would visit occasionally, they were called Mr and Mrs Riley. Their home was in North Wales. He would preach at our church but always insisted that he and his *dear wife* as he called her, would first "minister in song" this rather dubious description was open to interpretation. The rest of us called it something quite different. The problem with this "ministry in song" was the fact that neither of them could sing a note in tune, either on their own or with each other. My cousin Keith, who played the piano, told me that he had tried every key on the keyboard but still could not discover which one they were supposed to be singing in, as they swapped and changed so often. The couple themselves were totally oblivious of the musical mayhem they were creating and carried on regardless, eyes turned angelically heavenward, and singing with great gusto. The whole congregation shook with laughter, many stuffed handkerchiefs in their mouths trying desperately not to be too disrespectful.

You may be aware that as part of the Sunday morning worship in Pentecostal churches in those days, was a section called open worship, the congregation would be encouraged to use the gifts of the Holy Spirit. This would usually mean speaking in tongues, followed by interpretation or prophesy. They were also encouraged to pray publicly, so, when he or she had finished the prayer the rest of us would say amen and the next person would then stand up and contribute.

It was at this point that Mr. Tommy Woodhouse came into his own. He had a most poetic way of praying. He would always begin with the words: "we have wended our way from person's places and pastures, to come to this thy house oh God". As he stood to pray with eyes firmly closed and facing the front, in his enthusiasm he must have lost all sense of direction because his body began to slowly rotate in a clockwise manner. By the time he finished he was facing in a completely different direction from where he started. As children this was a source of great amusement to us, as we used to peep through our fingers.

Mr Woodhouse would sometimes be asked to take the communion tray containing the small glasses filled with grape juice round to the congregation.

As you may know the wine represents the blood of Jesus. Before proceeding with this solemn duty, he would always kneel before the communion table at the front of the church and recite a short prayer of confession about not being worthy or something. This confessional would not have been out of place in a High Anglican or Roman Catholic Church and said with a crucifix or Rosary in hand.

The little ritual of kneeling and confessing, greatly irritated Mr. Bill Murray, another member of the church. Bill was a staunch Northern Ireland protestant and hated anything that vaguely resembled Roman Catholicism.

Keeping the peace among some Christians can be tricky at times.

These days when a minister is invited to preach at an Elim church, they are usually accommodated in a local hotel or guest house but in those days, everyone stayed at our house. As a child I was fascinated listening to their discussions on the bible. The stories of answered prayer, the places they had been and the people they had met.

On one occasion as I was playing on the hearth with a magnet and some small particles of iron. A visiting preacher took my magnet from me and said, "I want to show you something David". He collected some ashes from the grate of the coal fire and buried the iron pieces in them. Now watch this he said, he lowered the magnet down to the pile of ashes, when the magnet got near to the ashes the particles of iron left the ashes and shot up to meet the magnet. This is what will happen when the Lord Jesus returns, he said to me, we will be caught up to meet the Lord in the air. I have never forgotten it.

My parents of course always financed this hospitality themselves. The church was small, and finance was small. The church treasurer at the time was also very small minded, and mean, so dad was not paid very much. Mother used to say the Lord always provides. We never went without the necessities of food and clothing but were quite poor in those days.

Our parents taught us never to swear or use bad language. But I wondered what it would be like to engage in this forbidden activity. So, when visiting my Aunt's farmhouse on one occasion I went into the dark cupboard under the stairs, where the cleaning brushes were kept, and secretly said a swear word, thinking that God would not see me in the darkness.

The farmhouse was the home of my uncle Alex and aunty Lillian He was the pastor of an Assembly of God church in Westhoughton in Greater Manchester, and he also had his share of unusual people. For instance, most Pentecostal churches in the 1950s and 1960s had a Saturday night meeting. It was called "Prayer, Praise and Testimony" night. These services were good for encouraging younger people to develop a speaking or preaching gift, but they also attracted several odd balls, miss-fits and weirdos who found an easy platform to expound their wacky ideas and unbelievable stories.

One man I remember regularly travelled from the nearby town of Bolton to give his testimony. At a specific point in the story, he would produce a large neatly pressed handkerchief which he ceremonially placed on the lectern explaining "I always weep when I come to this point". Whereupon he would take the neatly pressed handkerchief wipe the anticipated tear from his eyes, and after composing himself would continue with his story.

His friend gave testimony of how the Lord had healed him of a severed head, yes, a severed head! My uncle a very down to earth man who did not suffer fools gladly, remonstrated with him about this calling his story "ridiculous and fanciful and totally untrue", what is more he said, "it frightened the children". In reply he said to my uncle in a reassuring tone, "But it's true brother it's true!" Every man was called brother in Pentecostal churches in those days, and the women were called sister. Which was quite handy if you had forgotten their name.

Then there was Mrs Seddon she was a member of his congregation and was a stout lady of about sixty years of age. Whilst working with other members on a spring-cleaning day at the church building, her job was to clean the inside of the windows. She came across some splashes of dried on paint, no doubt left over from previous decorating attempts. Unable to remove the stubborn paint she said to my uncle "I'll leave it to the Lord!" I think it remained there until that building was demolished.

These and many other incidents, convinced me that the Christian ministry was certainly not for me. God, it seemed had other plans.

This is a little of my story. I believe that the ministry is a calling not just a job. I was working as a lithographic printing engineer in

Bolton at the time, I was very happy in the job and was engaged to Jean who came from the little village of Rishton some six or seven miles from Blackburn.

Through a series of strange events which I will not go into here I became increasingly aware that God was calling me into the Christian ministry. Things came to a head one Saturday evening at a convention we hosted.

Pastor Lesley Green was our guest preacher that weekend. His text for the Saturday evening meeting was from John's gospel. "Except a corn of wheat falls into the ground and dies it remains alone, but if it dies it brings forth much fruit." Although the verse originally referred to Jesus going to the cross, the preacher went on to say that if we too were willing to die to our plans, hopes and ambitions, from that "death" God would make something new begin to grow.

After taking my fiancé home I prayed that if God truly wanted me to train for the ministry, he would cause Mr Green to ask me about it as he was lodging at our house. In the morning, the first thing he said to me was, "David, have you ever thought of entering the ministry?" I bluffed my way out of it and said no; but the truth was that I had been thinking about it for some time. So, after several months of resisting the call, Jean and I postponed our wedding for a couple of years, and I applied to the Elim Bible College which at that time was situated in the little village of Capel in Surrey.

Chapter 2

Institutional life

I was late applying to the bible college and so could not start with the other students in October, but I did join the class the following January thus missing one term.

The principal and his wife were Pastor and Mrs Wesley Gilpin.

It was after being there for a few months that I learned of the five-year rule. The five-year rule meant that bible college students could not marry for five years without the express permission of the Executive Council, the ruling body of the Elim movement.

For two-year students like me this meant that after graduating you had to serve a further three years as a probationary pastor before the Executive Council gave you permission to marry. For three-year students this was reduced to two years' probation. Jean and I had promised the Lord that we would only marry after my two years training ended. So, because of the time it takes to plan a wedding I applied to the Executive Council at once and was duly denied permission. I learned later that the smart ones who were aware of this rule married before they came to college.

My college friend Stephen Hilliard lived in the Yorkshire town of Halifax and as we were both from the north we travelled together in his old banger of a car. I think it was an Austin 35 or a Morris Minor or something similar. However, it only had three of the four cylinders working. In January 1968 there was a large snow fall and only one lane of the motorway was cleared, Stephen didn't have the luxury of a heater in his car, so he and I chugged down to college at twenty five or thirty miles an hour in the freezing cold with nothing but a thin blanket to keep us warm. When we eventually arrived at Capel, we were roundly told off by the principal for coming late, the term had started the day before and we had not realized. Times were hard in those days.

Each student had a work period at seven thirty in the morning. My job was growing tomatoes when they were in season, feeding the plants and breaking off the side shoots. David Proven was a big Scottish lad, and he usually got more manual jobs to do. On one occasion he was felling a tree and cleared the area where it was to fall. The tree, on the other hand, had other ideas and fell the wrong way, breaking through the electricity power line and plunging the college into darkness. It was days before light was eventually restored.

I remember praying with him and a few others for another student who was ill.
We all went down below ground to an area known as The Ark, a favourite place of prayer for the students. After much crying out to God and storming the gates of heaven for the healing of this student, David boldly proclaimed that he felt we had broken through, and the student would now be on the mend. We all processed in joyful anticipation to his room on the top floor. When we arrived, the bed was empty, we thought he must be already dressed and walking about, but

unfortunately, he had taken a turn for the worst and had been taken to the hospital. Not the answer to prayer we were anticipating.

A lot of students like me could not get grants in those days. I had a small concessionary amount from our local authority, but this was only a token gesture, and didn't even cover a fraction of the college fees I needed to pay. We lived by faith and had to trust the Lord to supply our need.

One student I remember lived by faith and hints; he would write what he called his monthly prayer letter (we called it a begging letter). In this enticing document he would share in pathetic detail all his financial needs, just for prayer you understand. In this way cash seemed to flow his way more readily than it did to the rest of us.

I met several interesting people during my time at the college. Some entered the Elim ministry with us but only lasted a short time before going on to other things. Some joined other church denominations, still others like me continued to pastor churches in Elim right up to my retirement age and beyond. I have kept in touch with several of them over the years but sadly lost contact with most of the others.

Bible college students can be a mixed bag. One student I remember took photos of himself in the nude. There were no digital cameras in those days and so the photos were sent away by the local chemist to be exposed and developed somewhere else. When the developed photos came back, they were checked by the chemist. To his surprise and amazement, he found himself viewing exposures of a different sort! He no doubt wondered what kind of clientele had slipped into this institute of spiritual learning, and promptly reported the photos to the principal.

That student did not return the following year.

One of the more unconventional but inspiring lecturers was Wynne Lewis; where other lecturers had a glass of water at the podium, he always had a can of coke. I have forgotten his talks but vividly remember the rolled-up sleeves and the can of coke from which he would swig from time to time.

On one occasion he took us to Epson Downs on Derby Day. The Derby is the most famous flat race of the horse racing season. There were an estimated quarter of a million people on the downs that day. Wynne had a tape recorder and interviewed some of the punters whilst we had a pile of gospel tracts and tried to engage them in conversations spiritual. Not unsurprisingly they all seemed more interested in the racing than their soul's eternal destiny. I do not think we had any converts that day as far as the gospel is concerned.

I do, however, remember the race. I sat on the shoulders of the large Scottish student David, and we were close to the rails just by the winning post. Another student David Chamberlain was with us, in his unconverted days he had been quite an authority on the horses, understanding their form, and the odds connected with the betting. I remember thinking to myself that his love of the horse racing circuit might have spilled over into his new life in Christ.

The celebrated jockey Lester Piggot won that 1968 Derby with his horse "Sir Ivor". It was a thrilling experience to be there as the horses came thundering down towards the winning post, the noise of the crowd rising to fever pitch as they urged on their favourites.

The students in our year used to travel each Friday night to Brighton, back then nothing but a seaside town on the South coast. We would wander around the prom giving out gospel tracts and inviting people to the short service which was held in the Elim Church in a street called "The Lanes". On one such trip I engaged an older gentleman in conversation about his soul. He had obviously been drinking. Young man, he said to me in a rather condescending voice I have heard Torrey and Alexander. That event in his opinion seemed to trump anything that I may have to say to him.

Evangelist Dr R.A. Torrey and his song leader Charles M. Alexander were the finest gospel duo of their generation. They won thousands of men and women to Christ in America and here in Britain. I remember thinking to myself that this man on Brighton Promenade had heard the very best that heaven offered at the time and still he remained unrepentant.

Chapter 3

Freedom at last

I never thought the two years training would ever end, but eventually it did and in the autumn of 1968 I started as a probationary pastor.

In those days Elim Church probationers (now called Ministers in Training) were not placed as understudies to senior ministers but were immediately given a small church to look after. I think they worked on the principle that if you survived the first few years you could possibly make it in the ministry and if not, it was just tough luck.

At the bible college I was considered one of the more capable students of my year and was assigned to a larger church in Somerset. This was quite an honour at the time, and it was said to have a female millionaire in the congregation. So, I was looking forward to going. Whilst waiting for this appointment to materialise I was sent to Alloa in Scotland.

The church in the Candle Riggs area of the town was situated on the first floor. There were some two hundred hard wooden chairs in the auditorium with just five faithful followers sitting on them.

I asked these remaining few people if they would give me names and addresses of those who had attended in the past; and I set about visiting all of them. I must have contacted at least fifty people who each said that they would come back to that church if more people attended.

One mid-week bible study, a new person turned up out of the blue. Visitors were like gold in those days, and we tried to hang on to every one of them. His name was Mr Muir and he encouraged me with a verse of scripture; "It is good for a man to bear the yoke in his youth" he said. In my naivety I thought that he would now come and help build the church with us but that was the first and last time we saw him. He left the youth to bear the yoke on his own I'm afraid.

I decided to start a mid-week children's meeting and after just three weeks the attendance rose to over seventy kids. I was the door opener, piano player, the storyteller and the one who had to keep order for seventy exuberant children. My only helper was a single lady called May and she was totally blind.

I shall never forget the name of "Betty Mallet". She was a fourteen-year-old girl and rather large for her age. She kept shouting out in the meeting and generally being disruptive and disturbing the other children. In desperation I eventually frog marched her out of the building and locked the front door behind her. Only then was order restored. The order however was short lived as she now began throwing stones at the windows to the amusement of all the other children.

One cold October Sunday morning I went to the church early to light the coal fired boiler. When we arrived later for the service the place was filled with smoke. At first, I thought that the glory of God had fallen as it had done in the days of King Solomon but soon discovered that a cover plate for the chimney was missing and the smoke instead of going up the chimney had come out into the main building. Throughout the church service that followed everyone was coughing.

I stayed with a lovely couple called David and Jean Kay. They lived on Hill St. which as I remember was one of the flattest streets in town. She made the most amazing rhubarb and ginger jam. I have never tasted it's like before or since. I am ashamed to admit that I ate her whole winter supply in the three months or so that I was with them.

Chapter 4

My first church

The appointment to the church in Somerset that I was waiting for had fallen through for some reason, and I was sent to Hayes in Middlesex instead.

I would later learn that the five previous ministers had all left the ministry from that church. It seemed to be a launching pad out of the Elim ministry.
The pastor before me had lasted just six weeks – the story goes that he was there on Friday evening as large as life but failed to show up for the service on Sunday morning. It was later discovered for reasons best known to himself that Sandy (as he was called) had made a quick exit back to the highlands of Scotland. I did remember from his time in college that he constantly pined for his fiancé'.

Bob Horne was the pastor of the Elim church in Ealing and was also the District

Superintendent at the time. He decided that we should not have another induction service for the new minister. His reason being, that the last induction service was only six weeks ago. "We can't go through all that again". He said to me. As I walked through the front door of the church on my first Sunday morning the welcome person asked if I was visiting. I explained that I was in fact the new pastor.

Only two people had shown up for church the previous Sunday but when they heard that the church was getting yet another new minister other people were rounded up to attend. So, the final head count for my first Sunday morning service was fifteen people. Thus, instead of having the largest church of our student year I ended up with the smallest. This was my introduction to the full time Christian ministry. My dad said: "just use the time in Hayes as a training ground David; get some good sermons and study the Word for future ministry."

Looking through an old deacon's minute book was an education. It went something like this, brother so and so asked about the financial state of the church. The treasurer said that "the situation was grave". Next month, the financial situation is "very grave". The following month, the financial situation is "still grave". They fluctuated from grave to very grave for months on end.

Then there were several entries about a notice board. Brother so and so said that he would undertake to get a new notice board for the front of the church. Next month, brother so and so was asked about the progress of the notice board. He said, "that he hadn't got round to it as yet, but would do so from now on". The following month, brother so and so said "that he had been ever so busy and had not been able to get on with the notice board as yet".

I howled with laughter as I read the contortions of "legitimate" excuses this guy gave over the next few months for not completing this very simple task.

We were eventually given permission to marry by the Field Superintendent but had already fixed the date of our wedding as I felt the rule, certainly in our case, was very unfair. It was a left over from a bygone age and was rescinded shortly after this time.

Jean and I did however see some wonderful answers to prayer in those early days in Hayes, not least in the provision of somewhere to live. Weeks before we married, I had managed to secure two rooms in a house owned by a Mrs Satterthwaite. She was a dragon of a woman who charged us maximum rent for minimal accommodation. There was not even a fridge in the kitchen. After a few months of living there, however, she asked us to leave because her son wanted to move back into the rooms we occupied. Property was very hard to find at that time in West London and I searched everywhere without success.

At the conclusion of one midweek prayer meeting, a member of the congregation gave us a lift home in his car. He happened to mention that he had seen a fridge for sale and wanted to take us to view it. I explained that we could not afford one at the time, but he insisted. When I called at the flat where the fridge was for sale, the couple told me that it had already been sold.

I noticed however that they seemed to be leaving the property as there were several boxes and cases in the hallway. They were indeed leaving and moving into the RAF barracks at the nearby town of Uxbridge as he was an officer in the RAF. They gave me the phone number of the agency who leased those properties, and I rang them up and asked if we could rent that flat. In fact, I pestered them a little. We got the keys just one day before I had promised our *wonderful* landlady that we would be gone.

The little self-contained flat we moved into on Botwell Lane was a God Send. It had two bedrooms overlooking a beautiful park. There was a fruit tree in the garden and the rent was much cheaper than the two rooms we had had before.

The neighbours were amazed that we were able to obtain this property as they were very much sought after, with a waiting list of several years for them.
God can make a way where there is no way. We were very happy there. Both our girls were born in Hayes.

Things began to improve at the church and a few new people joined us. Having been married to Jean in March 1969 we seemed to attract other young couples of a similar age. Later, we all had babies at around the same time. This is what the church growth experts call biological growth.

In the book of Ruth in the bible the harvesters were told to drop handfuls of grain on purpose so that Ruth could gather them up with ease. These were little tokens of Boaz's love and care for Ruth. In the same way we too had little gifts of provision from the Lord at that time.

Shortly after Jean became pregnant with Rachel our first daughter, we needed a carry cot with transporter wheels. Money was scarce, we had just £5. A person at the factory where Jean worked said that she had a friend who was selling a carry cot, so we borrowed a car from one of the members and went to see it. Unfortunately, it was not suitable as it did not have any wheels with it. The lady, however, said that she knew someone else who did have what we needed and gave us the address.

The address she gave us proved to be the wrong one, as an elderly gentleman lived in that house. He did however tell us that there was a family in the same crescent that had young children and maybe it was they who had the cot for sale. We then enquired at this lady's house, but she too was not the person we were looking for, but as it happened, she did want to get rid of a carry cot with wheels herself. In conversation it turned out that they were a family of Christians who attended an Anglican church in Uxbridge she also said that she had a standing cot if we would like that as well. Everything was in perfect condition, and all for £5. She later wrote us a lovely letter saying that she had put the money into the missionary offering at their church.

Rachel was due to be born in early March 1970 but was late (a trait that has followed her through life). Jean's sister Mary came down specially to help at the time of the birth and she recommended Caster Oil to get things moving. Jean took a spoonful or two in coffee. In the early hours of the morning, she thought the baby was coming. I gave her my expert opinion that it was nothing more than a tummy pain brought on by the castor oil. When the pains continued, I changed my mind and went out to the telephone box at the corner of the street and phoned the hospital.

The ambulance, blue lights flashing, was with us in a few minutes and I helped Jean down the stairs and was about to get into the ambulance with her. The Para medic said that he would not advise me to go with them as the matron at the cottage hospital was an absolute dragon and would not let me stay there. Furthermore, they said we are not allowed to bring you back in the ambulance so it would be best if you stayed at home.

My wife gave me one of those looks which said, you are not going to abandon me in my hour of greatest need are you? I hopped into the ambulance, and we hurried off blue lights flashing to the small cottage hospital a few miles away.

The driver was right, the matron was a dragon, and would not let me stay. After safely delivering us into the care of this left-over relic from the Victorian Era, the ambulance drivers sped off into the night leaving me to walk the few miles back home in solitude.

At nine in the morning, I rang the hospital to ask how things were going and was surprised to learn that mother and daughter were both doing fine. There were however some problems with the baby's feet. On hearing this I was quite upset and worried. I then did something that I advise people not to do when seeking to find God's will or guidance on some decision of life. I looked at the bible verse printed on the calendar for that day. It happened to be from psalm 55:22 "cast thy burden upon the Lord and he shall sustain thee." It was a real comfort and reassurance at the time. I am less judgemental these days of promise box Christians, those who occasionally use the bible verse on the calendar or the bible reading plan in seeking God's will or direction.

Rachel's condition was later diagnosed as Talipes. At four days old she was fitted with brown boots to treat the problem in the early stages. Later in life she would have a couple of operations to lengthen the tendon and is perfectly well today.

On another occasion a lovely Baptist minister and his wife John and Catherine Eccleston regularly put money aside to give away as the Lord directed them. They kindly paid for us to attend our annual Elim Conference. By this time, the little carrycot was getting too small, and we needed a proper pram to get around. I knew we could get a second-hand pram for about £10 in those days, but we only had five.

As we were leaving the conference a pastor called Henry Postlethwaite from Whitehaven rushed over to Jean and put some money in her hand. It was a five-pound note just the amount we needed, so we were able to buy a lovely pram for our growing daughter Rachel.

I do not know if it is a northern thing, but we never locked our doors in those days. On returning home one day we discovered that someone had entered our flat. They had filled the whole kitchen with food. We never found out who had done this very kind act, but it was very much appreciated. One windy day I found an envelope in Rachel's pram with money in it. It had not blown away and was just enough for what we needed.

Jean and I rode bikes to get around the area and visit the congregation. We had a seat on the back for our daughter.

Seventeen months after Rachel was born our second daughter Esther came along, she was born early on Sunday morning at home in our flat; the midwife and I had been up all night with Jean and the new baby. About nine thirty in the morning, I walked the two miles or so to church, conducted the service and afterwards returned to our home. After the evening service I brought back the flowers that had been displayed in church for Jean. She did not need to know where they had come from!!

Chapter 5

More of the same

The church was still very small, and money was tight, but we had many wonderful provisions from the Lord. I well remember Eddy McAvoy coming to visit us. We made him a cup of tea with water boiled in the electric kettle. On leaving our upstairs flat he noticed that the gas meter was empty and promptly put a two-shilling piece in the meter for us. Little did he realise that we had absolutely no money to put in the meter that day. I had the joy of relating that story to Ed for the first time at his home in California some thirty years later.

On another occasion we had a missionary come to preach at the church. Jean bought one lamb chop and made a stew for our visitor and me (she is vegetarian). After the service, the preacher informed us that he would not be staying for lunch as he had made other arrangements. So, I had the whole lamb chop to myself.

The church building in Keith Rd in Hayes was situated right next to the railway line, and in those days some of the good's trains seemed to take an age chugging past the church and often drowning out the singing and preaching.

The building itself was in a dreadful state. It had been built several years before by a man called Pharaoh. I can categorically say that his standard of workmanship was nothing like his name's sake in ancient Egypt. It had a flat concrete roof covered with bitumen which melted in hot weather and dripped through the cracks.

The story goes, that years before, on a warm Easter Sunday morning a lady visiting the church for the first time was dressed in a new outfit. People would often buy new clothes at Easter, and she happened to sit down on a seat on which a newly arrived droplet of molten tar had landed, thus ruining her nice new Easter outfit forever. I do not think she returned.

After a while we set about bringing the building up to standard as it had been quite neglected. The roof had been fixed several years before but the walls on the inside were very damp and the plaster was falling off. It smelt very musty. We needed to erect an inner wall of bricks to create a cavity, as the present structure was a solid nine-inch wall. We employed a retired master builder to undertake the work for us. He was of the old school and did a fantastic job. Of course, I was the chief mortar mixer, scaffold erector, brick carrier and general dog's body. I can still remember the composition of the mortar to this day, four parts sand one of cement and a trowel full of lime.

All Elim churches pay ten percent to our headquarters, this is to run the administration of the movement and its many departments. It also pays for the removal costs of ministers. We were spending all the money we had on improving the structure of the building and inadvertently got about forty pounds behind in our payments to H/Q.

The field superintendent wrote a very threatening letter to me saying that my ordination would be put back if we did not pay. I must admit that I saw red and wrote an equally strong letter back, telling him that we had spent all the money on improving their building at no small cost to ourselves. I think he wrote quite a conciliatory letter in return - but still put my ordination back for a year. In the ministry you must try not to get bitter about injustice but realise that we serve the Lord not people.

I well remember the first baptism service I conducted. No one had been baptised in that church for over twenty years and so we had no idea how the Baptismal tank would hold up. We filled it with water on Saturday but by Sunday morning the water had all leaked away and the tank was completely empty. It took us all of Sunday afternoon to refill it again using a hose pipe and a convoy of kettles full of boiling water. At last, we were ready for the evening service.

A young lady by the name of Sheila was to be baptised. She was an attractive nineteen-year-old girl who attended another church but as they did not practice believer's baptism by total immersion she asked if we would do it. In my ignorance I omitted to tell her to wear something underneath the white baptismal robe we issued in those days, so when she emerged from the water soaking wet, she looked more like someone from a "Miss Wet Tee-Shirt" competition than a person raised to new life in Christ.

The first funeral service I ever conducted was for a Mr. Fuller. He did not attend very often but his wife did, and she was a lovely Christian lady. Our regular pianist Alan Masters was brilliant. His day job was playing piano for the dancers at the London Ballet School in Covent Garden, but of course he was not available during the day. Mr Barrett was our substitute pianist. By contrast, his style was, shall we say, different, to our regular pianist. Bill Barrett had perfected the art of the two-finger method of piano playing. Furthermore, he was also suffering from short term memory loss, and it came as no surprise when he forgot the funeral service altogether, so I had to play the hymns myself.

At the end of one Sunday evening service a stranger wandered in. He explained that he had had a date with a girl, but she had not turned up – so he had money to spare, to splash around. He said to me, "Do you accept cheques?" I tried not to appear too excited and said in a rather nonchalant manner that we did. He promptly took out his cheque book and wrote down the amount, briskly separating the cheque from the book he folded it neatly in half and handed it to me with the words "A few more of those and you'll be able to build yourselves a new church". I thanked him warmly and he disappeared into the night never to be seen again. I took the cheque to the treasurer but on route I could not resist having a little peek at the amount of our newfound wealth. When my eyes at last focussed on the figure we were due to receive it was the princely sum of ten shillings, fifty pence in today's money.

They say that the level of disappointment is the difference between what you hope to get and what you actually do get.

One Sunday morning Bob Widows turned up at church with his pregnant wife and their twelve children. It reminded me of the nursery rhyme.

> "There was an old woman who lived in a shoe. She had so many children she didn't know what to do, she gave them some broth without any bread and whipped them all soundly and put them to bed".

Unlike the woman in the poem however Mrs Widows was the calmest and most unflappable person you were ever likely to meet. When they all arrived in their minibus the congregation almost doubled.

They were with us for a year or two after baby number thirteen was born. Then one day the family came with the news that they were all emigrating to Australia. The church put on a grand farewell meal for them; we all wished them well and prayed that God would bless them in this exciting new venture on the other side of the world. So off they went.

Barely one year later there was a knock at my door and when I opened it there before me and to my great surprise was the smiling face of none other than Bob Widows. What on earth are you doing back? I asked, he said that they couldn't settle in Oz, so they were shipped back to Britain courtesy of the Australian government, apart from their eldest daughter who wanted to stay there. After returning home he had been able to purchase another vehicle – not a minibus this time but a two-seater Austin Metropolitan car. I suppose the kids had to walk.

Because their family was large, they had to be temporarily accommodated in two or three rooms at a women's refuge. I visited them there, kids would run in and out all the time and I had a job to decipher if the child that just came in was the same one as the one who had just gone out, as they all looked alike to me. Mrs Widows said that she just wanted one more baby and then her family would be complete.

The Field Superintendent Rev. Ron Chapman told us that they wanted us to leave Hayes and move to the north of England. He said that the church was larger, and it would be more suitable for us as a family. He would not tell me the exact name of the town we were assigned to until I had agreed to go. It turned out to be Macclesfield in Cheshire.

So, after almost five years we left Hayes. The church had now grown to about forty people by then. Although financially poor we had been very happy there and proved God to be our provider.

Chapter 6

Go North Young Man

It was 1972 that Jean and I and our two young girls set off for the north.
Macclesfield is famous for rain; and the week we arrived it poured down every single day. Rachel said to me "Daddy when can we go home?" I tried to explain that we were home. Moving can be tough on pastors' children.

Mr Bradley was the church secretary and he welcomed us by saying "I hope your stay here will be a long and happy one". I had known him since I was a boy, as my father used to preach at that church many years before.

Mr Bradley was, however, the first to leave us. It happened like this. As winter approached, we moved the prayer meeting from the main sanctuary to the minor hall next door. This minor hall was a large house that had been converted by knocking the two downstairs rooms into one. It seated about twenty people and was much warmer than the larger church building. Mr Bradley never accepted the minor hall as a place of prayer and worship, feeling that the only true place to petition the almighty was in the main sanctuary, so he left!! He had been a member of that church all his life.

The shape of the church building on Mill Lane resembled a double coffin. The manse where we lived was next door but one, so all and sundry used to call on us at any time of the day and night asking for the church key, information, or whatever.

This church had been in the doldrums for some years and so to get things moving again I decided to have a large evangelistic tent crusade.

Rev. Ray Belfield was an Assembly of God pastor in Wigan. His wife's parents lived in Macclesfield, and I often visited them. Ray had had a very successful crusade with an evangelist called Melvin Banks. So, on his advice I invited Melvin to conduct a tent mission for us. He insisted that we leaflet every home in the town twice over and extend the leaflet distribution to an eight-mile radius beyond the town itself. The leaflets advertising the mission were packed with photos and testimonials of miracles and healings that were said to have happened in previous missions.

We trudged the streets for weeks advertising the coming meetings. By the time the last of the 70,000 leaflets was distributed the suit I ordered from Burtons the tailors was two sizes too big.

We planned on having the tent erected in one area of the town for the first week, then moving it to another area for the second week; the third week was to be held in the church building itself. An intense three-week mission was quite an undertaking I thought.

Before the crusade was due to start, I made the mistake of visiting one of the trustees. He explained to me that they had tried all this kind of thing many times before and nothing had ever come of it. No one was ever saved, and no one was ever added to the church.

When I left his house, my heart was in my boots. Fortunately, God was with us, and we did see a number of people saved and added to the church.

The response from Melvin's advertising was amazing, people came from miles around. Melvin had the evangelistic gift of getting people to respond to the gospel invitation to become Christians. We had eleven hundred decisions for Christ in the three weeks mission; some people filling in the response forms five times over!! Long standing Christian's making sure they were saved for the umpteenth time!

Divine healing was a great emphasis of the campaign, and hundreds came just for prayer for physical healing. One man I remember had prayer for partial deafness, he also had two fingers missing on one hand. He lived in Half Street as I recall. The evangelist before praying for him and without bothering with his H's said, "you live in alf street do ya, you'll get more than alf yer earin"! On the way out the guy said to me, he is a wonderful man Mr Banks, and I believe before the end of the crusade he'll get my two fingers back as well.

One of my other responsibilities for the mission was erecting directional road signs and posting them all over town. On the changeover day I re-directed the signs to the new location but inadvertently forgot to change some of them, and so several visitors circled round and round the area several times trying to locate where this illusive tent mission was.

The Campaign cost us a fortune as Melvin was not cheap.
Besides the hire of the Tent, the removal cost, the cost of the advertising etc. he had us buy Ice cream and hot dogs for the teenagers and we provided food for the myriad of volunteer workers. He was also a little brash with some of the workers and I had to pour oil on the troubled waters on more than a few occasions.

The church treasurer was Mr. Gerald Clewes who some years earlier had opened a separate bank account which he called the "Little Extra Fund". He came to me after the crusade and with a forlorn look on his face he said that we had spent all the money in the general account and even the entire "little extra fund" has gone as well. This was the pits for him; no money; a treasurer's nightmare.

After the crusade ended, we bussed some of the new people into the Sunday services, and along with them were a few psychiatric cases as well. These were overweight ladies of a certain age and were residents of the local mental health hospital.

As an extra treat I would sometimes take two or three of them in my car to meetings out of town, I like to think that it brightened up their lives a little. The problem was that my car kept breaking down and they needed to get out of the back seat quickly and push. Having got the vehicle started they would then need to rush back and scramble into the rear seat of the car as quickly as possible while the engine was still running. It was the funniest sight to behold these overweight ladies running to catch up with the newly started car and scrambling back in. It took several minutes for them to get their breath back as they were all panting.

One of these ladies was called Irene. She was a lovely person - at least when she remembered to take her tablets. However, when she missed taking them for a day or two, she would imagine that she was getting married, and needed some "Going Away" clothes. She had a savings account and asked me to look after her bank book which I did.

One day she stormed into our house and demanded that I give the book back to her as she needed to buy clothes. I handed it over and she disappeared. Later that day, the sister from the hospital rang to inform me that she had gone missing. I explained what had happened and she told me that Irene would more than likely be on a bus going to Stockport. I quickly drove to the bus station and sure enough there she was patiently waiting for the bus to depart. I coaxed her off the bus by saying that I would take her to

Stockport in the car. Once in the car I explained that I had to take her back to the ward first to get something or other. She was not at all pleased, but I felt it was a justifiable piece of deception.

Like most Christian pastors, from time to time I receive words of thanks and appreciation from people I've been privileged to help along the way, but the compliment that sticks in my mind most vividly was paid to me in Macclesfield in the 1970s.

I would occasionally visit an elderly couple who lived close to the church. They did not attend our church and I think the wife's early years were spent in Southern Ireland. She had married an Englishman and settled here. To my knowledge they had no family, but they had a Mynah-bird that swore like a trooper. The wife assured me that it was him and not her that had taught it the rude words.

Eventually the old man died, and the widow asked if I would conduct the service because she said the local Roman Catholic Church was too expensive. Up to that point I had never considered myself a bargain basement funeral officiator, a kind of cut-price franchise in the dispatch department of the Church's ministry. As finance seemed to be an issue, I waived my fees and let them use the church building for free as well. After the service however she not only gave me a generous gift but paid me this compliment. "He could not have had a better funeral *even in Ireland"*.

Up to that point I was not aware that Ireland was the country of choice for funeral satisfaction. That compliment was paid to me over forty years ago and I still remember it to this day. Mark Twain said He could live two months on the strength of a good compliment.

Next door to the lady in question lived a young man called Bernard. He was a nice but naive young fella who had recurring mental health issues and had to be admitted to hospital from time to time. I would often go to visit him in hospital. When his mental health was improving, they would release him for the day. He would then need to return to the ward in the evening.

Late one evening he got someone to phone me to say that he was in a dreadful state, and he needed to get back to the ward. They said that he was so scared that he was hanging onto a lamp post and could not move as he was paralysed with fear. When I got to the supportive lamp post, there he was clinging to it for dear life. However, the moment I said, "get into the car Bernard," then he left his place of safety and hopped into the passenger seat. He seemed to have had a miraculous recovery, and by the time we reached our destination he was fine.
Reflecting on the incident later I thought to myself, I bet he made the whole thing up to save him walking back up the hill to the hospital.

One day I visited him at his home only to find that he was no longer alone in the house, quite the reverse, because several "ladies of the night" had moved into his place and taken over. As I entered the house, I think the girls looked at me as a potential client. Three weeks later however they all moved out again taking with them almost everything he owned and leaving him without even a plate or a cup, a knife or fork absolutely nothing, he was quite bereft.

On another occasion my wife Jean was tending the small garden at the front of the house when a lorry driver pulled up and with a wink asked if he could come in for a cup of coffee. When she refused, he continued to ask, and after another firm refusal he eventually drove off. It was only later that we discovered that the girl on the other side of our house was "on the game" and the driver had mistaken Jean for her. As you can see, we lived in a very classy neighbourhood in Macclesfield.

Another interesting person who came to our church occasionally was Doreen. She showed us a series of very upsetting and anonymous letters that she had received. They were all death threats, they described in detail what they were going to do to her, how they were going to kill her, and how they would get to her at a time she least expected etc. A further threat was that she was not under any circumstances to go to the police, it was very unnerving and frightening for her. We advised her to go to the police anyway, but she said that she was too scared to do so. She then received a bouquet of flowers with a sympathy note attached, "Rest in Peace" this will soon be you, or words to that effect.

After a while we ourselves started getting strange phone calls. The phone would ring but when we answered there would be silence at the other end. Sometime later the phone rang again and this time a heavily disguised female voice said that she knew people who were going to kill Doreen. We asked the usual questions. How do you know this and what are the names of these people? But no answer was forthcoming. After a couple more similar calls I had an uneasy feeling about these phone messages and thought that I recognised the voice of the person speaking, even though she was trying to disguise it.

Eventually we tumbled to it – it was Doreen herself, yes, she was writing the letters to herself, sending the flowers, and making the phone calls. Eventually I confronted her by saying "Come on Doreen we know it's you". She never admitted it, but the phone calls and death threats ceased after that.

Another strange lady came to the church in Macclesfield. She was very well educated but completely nutty. She carried her very small Chihuahua dog around in her handbag everywhere she went, church, shopping, everywhere. She told me that there were little demons blocking her hearing and asked me to cast them out. I thought that a bit of wax remover or something was a better solution.

Chapter 7

You're not supposed to laugh.

I remember getting the giggles at a funeral.

Whilst the undertakers were removing the coffin from the hearse Mr. Robinson our euphonium player, who had done a bit of everything in his lifetime informed me that he used to make coffins.

He complained to me that these modern caskets were not a patch on the old ones that he used to make. All they use on the handles nowadays, he said, are split pins. "We used nuts and bolts in my day – much stronger". As they were carrying the coffin down the aisle and I was walking ahead reading passages from the bible and trying to be dignified, I remembered Mr Robinson's words about the split pins, and had a vision of one of the handles falling off and the contents of the casket sprawled out on the floor. Imagination can be a terrible thing sometimes.

I also had another attack of the giggles whilst conducting a baptismal service. One of the candidates was a small lady in fact she was almost as broad as she was high. The water was very cold on that occasion and as she waded into the tank she gasped with shock as the cold water struck her legs. The expression of absolute shock and surprise on her face sent me into hysterics. I had to turn away as I was shaking so much.

The church building in Macclesfield had very good acoustics and whilst conducting a wedding ceremony the bride was overcome with emotion and began sobbing. The sobs got louder and louder reverberating round the building like the chimes of Big Ben. We had to wait several minutes for her to calm down.

On another day I visited a member of the congregation. She was a rather small single lady in her fifties or sixties. She was born with a serious curvature of the spine and had to wear a special corset. In conversation she informed me that she had now been fitted with a new corset. This new corset she explained had special bones and features which were not in the old one. She went on at great length extolling the virtues of this new aid.

On completing the account, she evidently felt that she still had not described the new garment adequately enough or in a manner befitting its superiority to the old one, not quite doing it justice so to speak. So, with a furtive look out of the window she said to me, "You are a married man aren't you"? Whereupon she promptly bent down, picked up her skirt and lifted it high above her head thus revealing the new improved special boned corset in all its majestic glory. As far as I can recall I believe I said that it was very nice and left it at that.

Chapter 8

The Big Apple

It was about this time that I was invited to preach at the Rock Church in New York. My dad had ministered there for several years, and now they asked if I would go also.

The Rock church had a constant flow of visiting ministers. You were expected to preach at least six times a week, and stay for a month, and they paid us well. Their senior pastor preached once a week on Sunday afternoon.

I shall never forget the first Sunday afternoon service. The senior Minister was Pastor Vick who was originally from Portland Oregon. He had been at the Rock Church for about thirty years. He stood up and addressed the congregation by saying. "Some of you are wondering why I haven't preached for the last six weeks – well, it's none of your business"! The crowd laughed as he explained that he had been doing a lot of reading and they would all get the benefit of his study in future messages. I thought to myself that you would not get away with that in the U.K.

Sister Abymacho was the choir leader at the time, and she gave testimony of how the Lord had miraculously healed her that week of cancerous lumps in her breast. All the lumps had completely gone. The surgeon who was due to perform the operation also attended the church. When she finished her story there was pandemonium. The congregation erupted in praise. Singing and praising God for hours. There was no preaching that day. only worship and song dancing and joy. I remember thinking how wonderful this was. I duly preached six times each week at the various services.

The church had a lot of great musicians, actors, dancers, and singers from the shows on Broadway. I would occasionally see someone on TV that I had seen in service the week before.

On one occasion I taught them a chorus entitled "I'm going to stay right under the Blood, where the devil can do me no harm". They loved it and sang it repeatedly. I had taken a small portable tape recorder with me, and I recorded their singing. I had to switch it off several times as the song went on and on and on.

I remember a ballet dancer swanning down from the balcony. She glided to the front of the church, did a couple of pirouettes, and then returned to her seat. Two men near the front who were not known for exuberant worship got out of their seats and did a highland fling at the front of the platform. There was such joy.

I loved the people there. The musical talent was exceptional; the choir, the solo and duet artists were amazing.

They also liked English preachers at the Rock Church. They called us all evangelists. We in Britain are much more comfortable exposing one-another's short-comings and faults. I found quite the reverse in New York. People upselling each other all the time.

They introduced me as our wonderful evangelist from England. Hearing that description about yourself each day for a month has a very therapeutic and positive effect on you. They of course called everyone wonderful, the wonderful choir, the wonderful musicians, the wonderful soloist. I scarcely found a person in the place who was not wonderful! They must have liked the boy from England as they invited me back the following year.

A Lady in our church in Macclesfield called Dorothy bought me a new light-coloured crimplene suit for the American trip; I felt pretty good in it and thought it looked great. Pastor Vick said to me "Brother Beresford (everyone was called brother or sister at the Rock church) Get yourself a nice dark suit when you come next year, it will look good against the light oak on the platform".

Another year I took Jean with me, and my mother looked after the girls.

The ladies on the platform all wore long dresses and Dorothy had given Jean a most beautiful long flowing green dress that she herself had made for the ballroom dancing competitions that she and her husband Bill entered. Jean felt like a million dollars. The ministers used to process in from the rear of the building to the platform when the service was due to start. The congregation would stand as we made our way to the platform. The people were so generous to us that they would rush up and put dollars in Jean's hand and my pockets as we walked down the aisle. I always told the pastor, but she smiled and said, "Just keep it".

Sister Annie Scirmont was the pastor who ran things on a day-to-day basis at The Church. One lunch time she took Jean and I out for a meal. "How would you like to come and be the pastor of this church?" she said. "You don't need to live in the city, you can live in New Jersey where it is more pleasant. You could also have two month's holiday a year to visit your family back in England". I was flattered, it was a very tempting offer, but Jean particularly was not so keen, and we felt that our heart was in our own country. We told her that we would pray about it but did not have peace about going.

I continued to visit each year in June for the next few years and into the 1980s. Dad always followed me in July. But then the format of the services became a little repetitive for me and I stopped going. Some things in life are for a season and that had been a great period of my life.

Chapter 9

A New Start

Although we had many wonderful and amusing incidents in Macclesfield and had seen the church grow considerably, Jean and I were never entirely happy there. Some of the new converts however were lovely and it was sad to leave them. So, after three years I asked our Headquarters for a move. They offered me Beeston in Nottingham. As I was uncertain whether to accept this church, I wrote to my dad who was preaching in New York at the time. I asked what he thought I should do. In those days, a letter took five days to get to the U.S. and the same to return.

Also, a friend called Peter who was in the Bible College with me was also living in Beeston and he happened to visit us in Macclesfield some weeks earlier. He was in the area with his new job, as the ministry had not worked out for him.

After just five days however a letter came back from dad saying he thought it would be a good thing to go to Beeston as he himself had ministered there some years previously. On the same day, a letter from Peter also arrived, this letter contained a cheque for £30. He had apparently sent it weeks earlier, but it had been returned for some reason, so he had resent it. The two letters arriving on the same day coupled with a sense of peace about leaving. We took all this as signs from the Lord that we were to make the move. So, we left Macclesfield and began our new ministry at the Elim church in Nether St. Beeston in Nottingham.

The church at the time was numerically smaller than the one in Macclesfield but from the very beginning it felt so right for us to be there. Just like a hand in a glove; I felt that this was somewhere I was destined to be. As I walked into the church building, I said to Jean that I felt that the building would soon be too small. She told me not to be so conceited. Some people have the knack of bringing you down to earth don't they! It might sound a little pretentious but after a few months of being there I thought to myself that I could not preach any better. I was free in my spirit and creative thoughts just poured into my head, and the church began to grow.

The building in Nether Street was originally a Baptist chapel; I think it was the oldest free chapel in town dating back to the 1830's. Before we arrived, the members had modernised the inside of the church. They sealed in the balcony and made the downstairs cosy and inviting. It had a disused graveyard in front of the main entrance and on one side of the plot stood a large blue wooden shed which was rotten with age, and which we flatteringly called "The Minor Hall".

It was about this time that our son Philip was born. The girls thought it was wonderful having a baby brother. He was ten pounds six ounces at birth and Jean had a real struggle. So, did I as a matter of fact, being the midwife's chief assistant.

Interesting characters seemed to attract themselves to us in those days. I well remember a Jamaican minister in full clerical garb turning up at an evening prayer meeting. He said that he had nowhere to stay and asked if he could kip down in the minor hall for the night. My better judgement said no, but as he appeared to be one of us, and in need, I reluctantly agreed.

When I went to see him the following day the hall was as hot as an oven. Every heater in the place was blasting out heat. He had also covered the blackboard with times and dates and flight numbers to various destinations around the world. This poor Jamaican pastor it would seem had an international ministry. More troubling for me however was that the entire surroundings had now taken on an air of permanence. He had brought a suitcase in from somewhere and showed absolutely no sign of leaving.

When I told him that he had to go he begged me to stay for one more night, assuring me that he had a place to live at Castle

Donnington, a small town a few miles away. The following day I packed his things in the car and headed towards Castle Donnington. Nearing the town, he said that he wanted to celebrate communion with me before we parted, I was reluctant, but my protests were in vain. He would not get out of the car until we had celebrated Holy Communion together.

Pentecostal churches never use alcoholic communion wine, so I called at the local Co-op and bought a loaf of bread to commemorate the body of Jesus, and because they had no Ribena, I had to be content with a bottle of orange juice to represent Christ's blood. So, he and I ceremoniously celebrated communion together in the front seats of my old Volvo car with Hovis bread and orange juice. Only then would he consider leaving.

He directed me to his former digs which were situated down a long farm track. We eventually came to some old stables where he told me to stop. I pulled up and he got out. I walked round the dilapidated buildings he called home and noticed that the walls were covered with flight times and flight numbers to many destinations around the world.

It was then that it dawned on me that this person was probably no more a minister than the man in the moon. He was more likely a psychiatric case or at the very least someone who was seriously deluded. We parted company and I never saw him again.

We soon demolished the old minor hall to make a carpark for the growing congregation. The late Charlie Stacy was an Elim pastor who used to be a lumberjack. I invited him to preach for us and to fell the large trees that grew on the side of the old graveyard. Charlie it must be said was a long-winded preacher and could be a little boring, but he was great tree feller and got them all down with ease.

We also engaged a local firm to level the ground for us. The heavy JCB digger they brought disturbed a lot of the brick-built graves beneath the surface. I returned from lunch one day to find the workers, or should I say grave robbers, looking for gold rings on the fingers of the long departed. Of course, I asked them to stop. Any treasure down there belonged to us.

Daisy was one of the more eccentric members of the congregation, a lady in her sixties who had never married. She had a stuffed life-size toy dog to keep her company and placed him in front of the window. "He likes it there sitting in the sunlight" she told me.

On one of the occasions that I visited her she said that she had just bought a pair of new blue knickers and asked if I would like to see them, I said, I would not but to my embarrassment she had already begun rolling up her skirt. I shall never forget the sight of those pale blue silk knickers with the elastic band gripping the thin leg just above the knee.

On another occasion she told me that people were breaking into her house, "Oh yes" she said, "they come in and take my things, and then a few hours later they bring them back but put them in all the wrong places". The personal forgetfulness explanation did not seem to occur to her.

I am told that a previous minister's wife went to see her after she failed to turn up for the Sunday morning service. As the pastor's wife had a key to the house, she let herself in, and found Daisy laid out on the bed dressed in her best night gown with a bandage tied round her head and chin and with two large pennies covering her eyes. On hearing Pauline coming into the room, she removed one of the pennies and said in a rather surprised voice "Oh It's you, I'm still alive". Apparently, she was convinced that she was about to die and did not want a man to see her naked, so she dressed herself ready for burial. Now that is forward thinking.

On a more positive note, she did buy the church a new organ.

I had preached about Mary anointing Jesus' body with the alabaster jar of fragrant oil. This took place a week before his death and resurrection. I made the point that Mary was the only one of his followers who anointed his body as the women who came to perform this task on Easter Sunday morning were too late, for Jesus had already risen by the time, they arrived at the tomb.

I then told the congregation that if they were going to do something for the Lord, they should do it now rather than later. To emphasise this point and by way of illustration, I said that there are some people who wish to leave the church some money in their will maybe to buy a new organ or something. Sadly, these people never have the joy of hearing their instrument played. Would it not have been better I said, if they had bought the organ while still alive? They could have heard it played and joined in the celebration of singing praises to God. "If you intend to give something like this why not do it now"? I concluded.

Daisy took this message personally and promptly said that she would like to buy the church a new organ. I went with her to the bank. She drew out £700 in cash which was a lot of money in those days. The bank manager was concerned seeing this frail old lady carrying so much money in her handbag accompanied by a strange looking man. I explained who I was, and we set off together to the music shop, which was just along the High Rd. She bought a nice instrument which brought a lot of pleasure to the congregation, and I am sure to the Lord himself.

A young man joined us from Nottingham. Some years before he had been involved in a serious car accident and spent much time in hospital, he was now recovering but was still in a lot of pain.

He was the kind of pseudo spiritual Christian that one encounters from time to time in churches. They have the knack of making the rest of us feel backslidden or at least sub-Christian. They see God's guidance in every small incident of their life. The church prayed for his continued recovery and after a while the pain subsided, and he felt a lot better.

He was now determined to get a job and applied for several positions. We all prayed much for him at every interview he had. I became his permanent chauffeur, escorting him for interviews all over the city.

At last, he got a job working in the stores at Nottingham University. Naturally, he was overjoyed as were the rest of us. The day of miracles had not passed. He proudly gave testimony to God's wonderful provision for him, and his face was radiant.

About three weeks later however he was downcast. The smile had completely gone from his face. The job, it seems, that God almighty had so graciously given him, was proving to be too difficult for him. Too much lifting was causing him a lot of pain. What was he to do?

He persevered for a while then one Sunday morning he turned up at church radiant. The familiar smile had returned to his face. He explained that he had been dismissed from his job in the stores; God it seems, in his infinite mercy had looked on his plight, seen his difficulties, and had got him the sack!

All now seemed to be going right for him again. However, when he arrived at the university on Monday morning, to work his one-week notice, he was dutifully informed by the Trade Union representative, that they had fought his case over the weekend. They felt that he was unfairly dismissed and had managed to get the decision reversed. They were now in the very happy position of telling him the good news, that he was reinstated in his old job. I don't think he was as happy as they were.

It is amazing how God changes his mind so frequently isn't it. I lost contact with his spiritual contortions after that.

I was once asked to visit an Iranian woman who was suffering with depression. When I arrived at the house, I discovered this lady was an attractive thirty-two-year-old. As I recall she was wearing hot pants (they were in fashion at the time). She had a husband and a young son. The husband was at work and her son was playing in the living room.

"I don't want to talk in front of the boy" she said "follow me" she led the way up the stairs to the bedroom. I innocently followed her like a lamb. She lay on the bed and began telling me all her troubles, these were mainly about the un- happy marriage that she was in. I sat on a high stool at the foot of the bed listening intently.

Call me naïve, but what will be clear to you as you read this account was not clear to me at the time.

Eventually however it dawned on me how this situation might look. Her lying on the bed, hot pants, and all, with me in the same room. If her husband came home, I am sure that I would be dead meat. So, I terminated the conversation as quickly as I could and then left.

There was also a young lady in our church who had very strange ideas about God's method of communicating with us. She was of Mediterranean extraction. She rang me one day in a very excited state. "Pastor" she said, "You must come down to my house de Lord has shown me something amazing you must come and see it". I went to her home later that day to see this amazing thing that the Lord had revealed.

She immediately took me into the kitchen and pointed to the back of the kitchen door. I stared at the door for a while but said nothing. She gave me a look which implied that I was missing something which to her was blatantly obvious. She continued pointing to the door then as if to give me a clue said, "De road! - de road! Can't you see de road? Her voice rising for emphasis. She explained, "Pastor, dat road was not there before, de Lord has put it there" she said.

The Sapele door in question had grain markings running from top to bottom. I suppose that with a little imagination you could have seen the outline of a road. Rather like recognising animal shapes or faces that one sees in the clouds sometimes. I told her that I thought it was just the way the grain ran. But she was adamant that the Lord put it there as a sign. What the sign was, or when he put it there, and for what reason, we will never know.

It was in Beeston that I forgot a funeral. Yes, after everything I said about Mr. Barret in Hayes and his bad memory, and he failing to turn up to play the piano at a funeral there.

I was asked to conduct a cremation service for a lady I did not know. The undertaker told me that ours was the first on the list, nine-o-clock in the morning. I remember thinking to myself, "I bet I forget that". Ten past nine on the morning of the funeral the undertaker rang to ask where I was. I was absolutely mortified. The funeral had gone completely out of my mind. Jean had taken the car to the shops, Barbara, who lived across the road had also left. I was totally on my own and without transport. I have never experienced panic like it in all my life before or since. I just froze and did not know what to do.

The undertaker sent his car to collect me, and they slotted us in after the following service had ended. The vicar conducting that service said, people will forgive you for forgetting a wedding, they will forgive you for a christening, but they will never forgive you for forgetting a funeral. This as I recall was not very comforting at the time. I of course apologised profusely to the family. The rather small group of mourners however were very kind to me and said, "It's just like old Doris, she was late for everything"! I thought it best not to attend the wake afterwards.

Chapter 10

No pain, no gain

Pain and pleasure often go together, and the Christian ministry is no exemption.

We had been in Beeston for about four years; the little building though cosy was now hopelessly inadequate to accommodate the growing congregation. I well remember a young couple turning up a little late for one of the services. They could not find a seat as people were crowded even into the foyer area and blocking the entrance, so this couple turned round and went home.

There was a church in town called The Gospel Mission. They had a building much larger than our own. Historically this mission had done a lot of good work in the town particularly among the disadvantaged children. At present they had no pastor, furthermore a group of younger members had left the church to start a new fellowship of their own. It was a very painful time for the faithful few who remained. The small congregation was now reduced to mainly elderly people and was in decline. We had always had a good relationship with them, and it occurred to me that if we merged with this church, it could be the answer for both congregations.

I prayed much about it and sought the Lord for guidance. The leaders of our church also prayed and were in favour of the proposition. One particular week as I was seeking God about the matter, I remember seeing someone from the Gospel Mission every day of that week. This gave me hope that we were on the right track. So, I visited one of their leaders and put my thoughts to him. He also felt that it could well be from the Lord, and so we got the ball rolling.

A series of meetings took place and eventually it was decided that we would take over their church. They were willing to give our denomination everything they owned, the building and all the money they had in the bank to help modernise the rather neglected structure. We began Sunday services in the larger but basic Gospel Mission situated in Willoughby St.

All was going well until two of my leadership team got cold feet. They did not want to leave the cosy little building they had been used to, and several of our original congregation felt the same way. They also felt that these evangelical Christians at the Gospel Mission were not Pentecostal enough and would stifle the freedom of the Spirit that we had been used to.

One lady told me that she had found Christ in our existing small building. She was baptised there and would like to be buried there. I thought how spiritually ambitious she was. Furthermore, they had had a prophetic word from a visiting preacher some years earlier saying that "In ***this place*** I will bless you". Thus, some of my original congregation felt that God's blessing was only for that building. I felt that God had indeed fulfilled his promise, as we were at capacity in the small building and needed to expand. There was also a bit of an ongoing power struggle in our leadership group that had not been successfully dealt with.

A series of church business meetings was convened and chaired by members of our Executive Council. The Charity commissioners were also involved and gave us their ruling.

To cut a long and very painful story short, a group of about thirty-five of our original congregation led by two deacons in my leadership team won the right to remain in the small building and continue with services on their own if they so wished. The rest of us moved to the Gospel Mission without them, and eventually renaming it The Oasis Christian Centre.

The first Sunday we started at the new venue the offerings rose by eighty pounds a week. Within one month sixteen new people joined us and the church began to steadily grow. Above and beyond all that, there was a real sense of the presence of the Lord in the meetings. Although we had left several people behind who didn't want to come, those of us who took the step of faith had unity and were seeing God's evident approval of this move.

After a while we set about modernising the old mission building. We constructed inside toilets; a soundproof baby room was built, and we also erected a balcony to accommodate future growth. This was in 1981.

Later we built a new secondary Hall at the rear for Sunday school and other activities. We also opened a café on Fridays for people shopping in town. We then purchased land at the side of the church. This land and the cottage that stood on it was owned by a very large lady.
She was also an avid CB enthusiast and spent all her days and nights parked on the settee conversing with other CB enthusiasts. These conversations in all their intriguing detail frequently broke through our sound system at the Sunday evening service. At the most inappropriate time's taxi cabs would be ordered with people needing to be picked up

from various places. We were not spared any of the details.

However, those meetings in the eighties were some of the most blessed and productive I have ever experienced, in a few years this building also was packed to capacity. The sense of God's presence at that time was wonderful. It was just great to be in church.

I well remember one Sunday morning service. The Church was packed, and the music was loud, it was warm and there were bodies everywhere. One of the old Gospel Mission leaders called Eddy Sanders who preferred things quieter and more orderly in church said to me, "David, we prayed for this for years". Even though I knew it was not his style of service he recognised the presence and work of God, and was very pleased to go along with us.

Chapter 11

Fresh faces

Shortly after moving into the new building a few discouraged and unhappy members from the nearby town of Long Eaton began to visit our church. In the interest of good inter pastoral relationships I rang the pastor to inform him that they were attending. He responded by saying "You're welcome to them David they are nothing but trouble".

At first, they all looked rather down in the mouth but after a few weeks of attending their joy and laughter returned and they became some of our very best members.

I well remember being asked to visit a couple from this group who said they were having problems in their marriage. I asked when they first noticed the difficulties. To my surprise they said that it was when they first came to our church in Beeston. When I quizzed them further, they told me that when they were members at their previous church everyone was miserable and unhappy, and they felt that this was quite normal. However, when they started attending our church they said everyone seemed happy and couples were holding hands and laughing. It was then that they realised that they had problems.

Long before the advent of the book "Fifty Shades of Grey" a young lady came to the church that I later discovered was a dominatrix. Apparently, she used to dress up in all kinds of kinky clothes and smack people with a whip or some other object (even though they had done nothing wrong!). After she gave her life to Christ, she left all that life behind.

She was a trusting sort of person and I thought that she was quite vulnerable. She took a real liking to me and to be honest I rather liked her as well, in a pastoral sense you understand! I think she looked at me as a kind of father figure in Christ. At some point she must have gone back to her old friends and told them all the things that had happened to her. How she had found the lord and the church and the nice pastor that helped change her life.

A few weeks after this, the phone rang in our front room and when I answered a female voice started asking me all sorts of intimate questions and making very suggestive sexual overtures to me. When I asked who was speaking, she promptly hung up. I returned to Jean who was in the living room and told her with a rather mischievous grin on my face. "I think I've just had a dirty phone call". I never knew who it was that rang but my feelings told me that it was one of the young lady's old friends in the sex trade.

Annette Richmond had been a member of the church for years. Her day job involved assessing and caring for vulnerable children, but she felt the call of God to the ministry and was accepted at our bible college. Regents Theological College, which was then situated at Nantwich in Cheshire.

When she returned after three years there was no opening for her on the paid staff at the

Oasis as Dave Newman and I were the only paid ministers. Annette served the church, however, working with the children's ministry and supporting herself financially. With the increase in finance, it then became possible for us to bring her on the paid staff as an associate minister and she was a real blessing and did a tremendous job for the Lord.

By the late eighties, the group from Long Eaton had grown considerably with people bringing their friends and neighbours along. We decided that the time was right to start a Sunday evening meeting in the now disused Elim church building there. They would still be very much a part of our church by coming to Beeston for the morning service.

But after almost a year the evenings in Long Eaton were not going well. There was not the same atmosphere, and the people were discouraged. We gathered our leadership team together and decided to book a country retreat centre for a day of fasting and prayer, asking the Lord what we should do. At the end of the day, it was decided to bring everyone back to

Beeston for the evening service and continue as we were before.

On the way home however, I felt that we had made the wrong decision. Jean said, "Oh no you've done it again". One of the things that I had been criticised for over the years was changing decisions agreed by the deacons. But the Lord spoke to me from a passage in Luke 13. Jesus told the story of a vineyard owner that had a fig tree planted in his vineyard, but this tree had not produced fruit for three years. "Cut it down" the owner said to the gardener, but the gardener responded. "Keep it one more year, I'll dig around it and fertilise it and if after that there are no figs then we'll cut it down". I felt that God was saying, give it our best shot and continue the evening services in Long Eaton for another year.

A young bible college student called Michael Williams was assigned to our church from the Bible College and had been with us for over a year. It became possible for him to join our team as a probationary minister because pastor Dave Newman had moved on to a National Role heading up the youth department of our movement.

I gave Michael the responsibility of looking after the evening congregation at Long Eaton. The rest as they say is history. He liked them and they liked him. The congregation began to grow under his ministry. So, we planted the remaining eighty members who were coming to Beeston in the morning, back to Long Eaton. I think at its peak that congregation with Michael as the pastor reached about four hundred and fifty people.

We of course at Beeston lost eighty of our congregation all at once. I told my associate minister Annette, that the finance would most probably drop considerably and that both of us may well have to take a cut in salary for a while, she said that she was fine with that. However, to my amazement the weekly offering rose, it was amazing, and within three months the church was again packed out. It showed me that when you do something that pleases God, he always looks after you as well.

Chapter 12

The times, they are a changing

Our Head Quarters had asked me on several occasions to move from Beeston and take on different roles within our denomination. A Regional Superintendents job and various larger churches were offered to me, but I never felt it right to accept. After a while however I began to wonder if God was saying that it was time for a change.

I attended a minister's meeting at our bible college and two senior leaders of our denomination Rev Wynne Lewis and Rev Gordon Hills asked if I would consider going to Plymouth for an interview. Plymouth had been a very large church in the late eighties but was now in serious decline and they thought that I was just the person to stop the rot and build the church back up again.

After much heart searching and prayer, I decided that nothing could be lost by going for an interview. So, on March 24th, 1994, my fiftieth birthday, Jean and I went down to Plymouth to meet the Elders. It was a wet and miserable day, and I had a headache. The large church building still had those old-fashioned pews and it felt like a barn of a place, and seriously in need of upgrading. The church I found out later also had a large debt. On returning home I was certain that we would not be going to Plymouth.

A few days after our interview the elders rang me and invited me to be the pastor and I told them that we would pray about it and let them know.

Many thoughts crossed my mind at that period of my life. First there was a prophet from Penang who said to me some years earlier that I would need a real word from God to leave Beeston. Then there was the consideration that we needed a larger building.

A building had come on the market called Falcon House, but which would need a lot of money spending on it to make it fit for church services and ministry. My leaders were less keen than I was. While we were considering whether to put an offer on this building, we were told by the council that the large public car park across the road from Falcon House would not be available to us as it would be closed on Sundays. We would have to provide adequate parking for the congregation on site and so would need to purchase extra land adjacent to the building in question. This would incur an additional cost of £100.000, which seemed an awful lot of money then. Did I want to start a massive building project and the financial commitment it would take at my age? Furthermore, my leaders were not wholeheartedly behind it. To be honest I was also a little battle weary. I had been in Beeston for almost twenty years. If I was ever going to move this might be the right time.

Chapter 13

By the seaside

Coming to Plymouth was not an easy decision and I had not the same spiritual guidance and confirmation that had led me to Beeston twenty years earlier. Sometimes you must just pray about things and make the decision and trust that God will show you if it is a wrong move. The old verse from the book of Proverbs is always relevant "In all your ways acknowledge him and he will direct your paths".

Leaving Beeston was a wrench and a loss. I did not realise the effect that loss would have on me, and I did not realise that I had experienced loss. Only looking back can I now see the losses that then occurred in my life.

In 1992 our two daughters married and moved away from home. In the same year, my mother died. Then in 1994 we left Beeston after almost twenty years to come to

Plymouth. In Beeston we had a good standing and reputation in the town but in Plymouth we had nothing, no one knew us; It was as if we were starting from scratch all over again.

When we came to Plymouth, I felt that God gave me a verse from Joshua 1:6. "Be strong and courageous because you will lead these people to inherit the land, I swore to their forefathers to give them." My feeling was that God had made promises of something great for this church but somehow in the past they had missed it, but God now wanted to restore it.

The Plymouth Christian Centre had been one of the largest churches in the city. Pastor Maldwyn Jones had moved them from the small building in Knott St. to the much larger premises in Embankment Rd. Under Maldwyn's ministry and later Pastor John Smyth the church had experienced a real touch of blessing and revival. There were conversions every week, and the church was packed out.

After Maldwyn left and a few years later John had also left, it must be said that both left prematurely, and the church began to decline. Another minister Pastor Barry Killick stayed just two years and still the church was declining.

Headquarters had asked me to go to Plymouth and try and get the church back on track, claiming that I was just the man for the job. For my part I felt like a lamb to the slaughter.

Instead of me leading the church back into growth, the decline accelerated with people leaving all the time. In the first eighteen months of us being there, eighty-one people left with their jobs – they just moved out of town. Others left for different reasons. In one month, some people left because they said that the Toronto blessing, which was sweeping through many churches at the time, had not come to our church because God himself had left us. But counter wise others left because they said that the Toronto blessing had come to our church and in their opinion, it was not of God anyway.

I shall never forget the first extended leaders meeting we held at Catchfrench Manor in Cornwall. It was all out war, so much hostility and disunity so much distrust in the Elders. One elder's wife ran out of the room in tears because of the criticism against her husband. My wife went to comfort her. Christians can be very unlike Christ at times.

Besides the large debt the church carried (the origin of which was a mystery); I also discovered that the church was being sued by a person from our nursery for unfair dismissal; a figure of £40,000 compensation was mentioned. Eventually a much smaller amount was agreed, in an "out of court" settlement, on the condition that the Elders apologise publicly to the whole church. This they duly did at the conclusion of a Sunday morning service.

The apology was read out by the administrator on behalf of the elders, but this was not sufficient for the family who stood up at the end of the service and shouted demands that each elder apologise separately and personally. There was chaos. I had some sympathy with the claimant's case but not the way they all handled it. I was not used to this public display of bad manners.

I continued to preach the best I could and to do all the usual pastoral work but still the congregation declined. Worse still, I could not see growth in my spirit.
To say I was unhappy was an understatement. My oft repeated prayer at that time was "Lord please help me to like this town". I thought that I had made the biggest mistake of my life.

We began to remove the pews from the downstairs area so that we could use that space for other events on weekdays, but I still felt that I was getting nowhere. The church members however were wonderful. They were kind, sympathetic and encouraged us to keep going, assuring us that it takes time for a large ship to turn around.

In 1996 we returned from holiday on the Isle of White and I prayed on the way home,

"Lord, would you give me an honourable way out".

The following Monday our general superintendent Wynne Lewis (yes, the same one) rang to ask if I would let my name go forward for the Regional Superintendents job in the North of England, other members of the executive council phoned me with the same request. I felt that God had indeed heard my prayer and was giving me a way out, a choice. I was relieved and did not feel quite so trapped.

After a couple of weeks however I began to think differently. I felt that if I left the church at this point having been here for just two years, and with the refurbishing in its early stage it may just discourage the very people who had faithfully stuck with us through the difficulties and destroy the church completely.

It was then that the Lord highlighted for me a verse from Philippians 1:23-24.
The apostle said, "I am torn between the two; I desire to depart and be with Christ (I didn't

go that far) which is better by far, but it is more necessary for you that I remain in the body. Convinced of this I know that I will remain and will continue with you all for your progress and joy in the faith". I felt that God was giving me the choice.

With that in mind and after much heart searching, we decided to stay in Plymouth. I well remember a person visiting us from Rev. Colin Urquhart's church in Horsham. He wrote me a prophetic word that went something like this. The path you have chosen was the more difficult one, but it was the right one; it went on to say that future blessing would follow.

Although the church was not growing there was a much better atmosphere among us and people began to trust the leaders more. There were not the same demands to know where every penny was spent because we had been transparent with everyone. I could not see numerical growth in my spirit at that point, but I could see more unity and understanding, with people getting on with each other much better. I have always believed that church growth is an atmosphere.

We bumbled along the bottom so to speak for a year or two. Not needing to use the balcony of the church as we only had a weekly attendance of about a hundred and fifty people. A shadow of what it once was at its height.
Eventually God began to add to our numbers, people were saved, others joined us and things began to look up. One lady from out of town joined us for several months and really blessed us financially which was a great help.

Chapter 14

Geoff and Jenny

Before recalling some more unusual incidents and interesting people, I would like to tell you how Geoff and Jenny came to Plymouth, Geoff is now the senior pastor here.

I have also omitted to mention the many things that caused the church to grow in the following years, such as our Kidz Klub programme and other initiatives. At one stage we needed two morning services for a time to accommodate everyone.

To return to my story, Geoff had been part of our church in Beeston whilst studying as a student at Nottingham University. His ministry had always been blessed and he led several fellow students to Christ. Things seem to happen when he preached. I wanted him to become an assistant pastor with me in Beeston, but he declined as he felt led to go to Cologne in Germany. This was the church he had attended whilst studying for his degree in languages. He had also taken a shine to the pastor's daughter there, which I am sure had absolutely nothing to do with his wanting to return!

Whilst I was still in Beeston, I felt that God gave me a verse regarding Geoff from the little book of Philemon verse 15 "Maybe he has departed from you for a season that he may be with you forever". I had completely forgotten this verse after coming to Plymouth.

Our paths had not crossed for years but he did invite us to his and Jenny's wedding, but we were unfortunately unable to attend. Then out of the blue he rang me from Germany as he had lost our address. As we talked, I asked him if he would come over to Plymouth and be the Youth Pastor here. He explained that things had gone a little pear shaped for him and Jenny in Germany and that he was not the person we knew in Beeston. He also said that they were thinking of enrolling at Kensington Temple Bible College in London for a year to get their lives back on track.

However, as we talked an incident from the book of Acts came forcibly to my mind. It was the time shortly after Saul of Tarsus had been converted. He had returned to Tarsus, his hometown. This town was miles away from where the spiritual action was taking place, it was a kind of backwater. Saul was not really involved in anything that God was doing in the wider church. Barnabas however went to Tarsus and brought him back, not to Jerusalem, but to the newly formed church in Antioch. As we continued to talk, I felt that I was being a bit like Barnabas helping Geoff to get back into the ministry and the place where God wanted him to be.

He said that he would pray about this and let me know. Within a short while he wrote back thanking me for the offer but declined saying that he and Jenny did not feel it right to come at that time. However, the very same day that the letter arrived he rang saying that they had had a change of heart. They were now willing to come over for an interview and take things from there.

They met the Elders and found that they liked the city and decided to come on board as the Youth Pastor. The rest as they say is history.

Chapter 15

And finally...

When I first came to Plymouth in 1994 the congregation was not used to my sense of humour. I remember addressing the candidates at a baptism service on one occasion. I told them that they had nothing to fear going under the water as I had baptised hundreds of people over the years and in all that time had only ever lost one. After the service, a lady came to my wife and said that it was a pity about the one, he lost. She had to explain to her that it was just a joke.

We have had our share of strange people in Plymouth. A guy called Chris used to turn up out of the blue from time to time, he was a sniffer and a drinker, he would creep up behind the ladies and sniff them. Not surprisingly they were not at all pleased, especially Marlene the secretary, we had to warn him about his behaviour on several occasions. He was a traveller and went from place to place with his rucksack on his back, and he always wanted money to get to the next destination. We had been caught so many times with these kinds of people that we decided the church would not give any more money to them as they usually only wanted it for booze.

One Sunday morning Chris turned up at the end of the service saying that he needed to get to Totnes urgently. Again, and again he insisted that he needed to get there. I was left with him when most of the congregation had gone home. In fact, as I recall I was usually the one who was left to deal with the difficult characters. Chris continued pressing me for cash to get him to Totnes. I was adamant he was not getting any more of the church's money.

David Isaacs was standing next to me and said in a very cheerful voice, "Pastor, I'll take him to Totnes myself right now". I watched Chris's face, his countenance fell, as he really did not want to go to Totnes at all. He just wanted money for booze but what could he say to the generous offer that was just made to him? Reluctantly, he got into the car and was driven to a town he did not want to go to, this amused me no end. Before getting out however he still asked Dave for money.

The first Sunday evening service of the New Year 1996 I decided to have a testimony meeting. I invited the congregation to share their most significant experience of the Old Year. One young man who popped in from time to time was the first to contribute. Not being a regular member and feeling he had to justify his spiritual pedigree he began by saying, "I am one third Pentecostal, one third Catholic, and one third Buddhist".

This was not enough; more was to come. He said that the most spiritual time for him in the previous year was at the special services that a few churches had organised in the Guild Hall. It was wonderful, he said. People were falling under the power of God, others were crying, some laughing, and nobody was taking the p**s. When he said the P word, I wished the floor would swallow me up. This was not the language of Zion I had been used to hearing. We vetted testimonies for a while after that.

I once went to visit a young mother who had just given birth, she was in the maternity ward of our local hospital. It was around lunch time. All the family were present, the husband and parents all wanting to see and hold the new arrival.

There is heightened security at maternity wards these days. I explained to the sister that I was the pastor. She then took me in to meet the family mistakenly saying, "the Pasta is here". The young mother replied, "but I ordered pizza". On seeing me they all collapsed with laughter. I have been called many things in my time but never a pizza.

On another occasion Geoff and I went to pray for a man who was sick and depressed. We spoke with him for a while about his problems and the need to give his life to Christ, and find the peace that Christ brings when we believe. We prayed with him in his kitchen, as I remember it was a solemn moment. However, whilst quietly petitioning the almighty on his behalf, lights flashed, and the whole house burst forth with a deafening sound of alarm bells ringing. It seemed that during our short prayer I had inadvertently leaned back against the panic button in his kitchen, thus setting off his entire alarm system. We left before any security people arrived.

One of the funniest incidents I have ever witnessed in the ministry happened here in Plymouth. A member of our congregation died rather suddenly. He was a man who enjoyed lots of fun and was a great practical joker. Sometime after his cremation the undertaker gave the widow a large plastic urn containing his ashes, she asked if I would conduct a short service and scatter these ashes.
The place they chose to scatter them was a local beauty spot where the deceased along with his brother and friends used to play as children. It is a beautiful, picturesque area, a river winding its way through rambling woods and soft grassy banks.

We arrived in a convoy of cars and parked in the car park near the edge of the forest. As we walked along the family reminisced about the fun, they all had as children, playing hide and seek and climbing trees in these beautiful surroundings.

After a while I gathered the mourners together on the bank of the river, read a few familiar passages from the bible and thanked God for the life that had now passed and prayed for the comfort and peace of God to rest upon the family. After this short ceremony I invited the widow to choose somewhere to scatter the ashes.

She had already decided on scattering them in the river so, kicking off her shoes she waded out into the cold quickly flowing stream clutching the plastic urn. The initial shake was beautifully executed, and she dispensed with about sixty percent of the contents.

She then became more adventurous, wanting to complete the task a little further into the river. As I watched her, I remember thinking to myself that she was moving rather quickly for such a solemn occasion. As she explained later, she had slipped on a stone and was frantically trying to keep her balance. This as it turned out proved to be futile and she was projected face down into the fast-flowing river. Before hitting the water however, and in an effort to protect herself, she inadvertently let go of the urn. The urn, now free from its captive mooring and only forty percent full of its contents, stood upright like a cork in the water and began to float majestically downstream. The final remains of the dearly departed were indeed departing much quicker than any of us had anticipated.

The ashes may even have reached the sea were it not for the quick thinking of his son who ran into the water wearing his new suit and shoes and recaptured the runaway urn. Meanwhile the widow sprawled out on all fours in the river was desperately trying to stagger to her feet hysterical with laughter. All of us were laughing uncontrollably. It took several minutes for us to regain any sense of composure.

She eventually dispensed with the remaining ashes whilst dripping wet and still laughing. Later she called it the "Joy of the Lord". On the way back through the woods the deceased brother said that if he hadn't known any better, he would have sworn his brother had pushed her into the water on purpose. He was such a joker.

Later that afternoon the widow rang to ask if I could remember the song her late husband had requested at his baptism some three years earlier – but I could not remember. She told me it was the song "Take me to the river". Well, he certainly got his request. All in all, it was the happiest, funniest, and most joyous ashes scattering service I have ever conducted.

Well, I think that's just about it for now I've almost finished my meandering through some of the incidents of my life and the more unusual people that I've met along the way and the fun we have had.

Of course, there were thousands of other wonderful people that have enriched and blessed us. Some are still with us, but the majority have sadly left us and gone home to their reward in glory. We shall see them again one day.

I have also omitted a lot of the more serious difficulties that we have encountered and the struggles that we have had. I did not want to burden you with these as you may have enough trouble of your own. I have also omitted telling you of the many times that God spoke to us through personal words of guidance and encouragement.

I have now been semi-retired since 2009 and Geoff Lee has been the senior minister at Plymouth Christian Centre since then. Paul Wright is the associate minister. You never retire from the Lord's work, but I hope to retire from the church team completely in March 2024. We had to adapt to a different way of doing church during the recent pandemic of Covid 19. It proved to be a growth factor for us, as we now have our own YouTube channel where people can watch online before coming into the centre.

The church continues to grow under Geoff's ministry and as I write it is thrilling to see the joy and excitement which we all feel.

The Sunday morning service is packed out. The Alpha courses are well attended by people wanting to know more about the Lord Jesus.

Our children and youth work seems to get better and better with our dedicated staff.

We all want the Plymouth Christian Centre to be a significant force for good and for God in this city.

Shortly after taking over from me in 2009, Geoff invited our daughter Rachel with husband Hamish and the family to come to Plymouth and take on the role of youth pastors. I was a little apprehensive at the time because they were so happy in Southport where they lived. I did not want their children to suffer in the ministry by being uprooted from their friends. I need not have worried. Now they are all settled in Plymouth. Hamish and Rachel have done a wonderful job among the young people. It is also good for Jean and me to have all the family nearby.

Our middle daughter Esther is the community pastor at the Baptist church in St. Austell and is fully involved in the Lord's work. She is also a semi-professional singer doing gigs in Devon and Cornwall from time to time. She also goes out busking, complete with woollen gloves, furry hat, and scarf in cold weather.

Our son Phil is going on with God and is a self-employed cabinet maker and joiner. We are so grateful to God that all our children and many of our grandchildren are following the Lord.

Even though the early years in Plymouth were very difficult for Jean and me, she has stood with me though it all, for which I am truly grateful. We have had many wonderful and personal blessings here. God has been at work in so many lives over the years, and the

Plymouth Christian Centre has grown into a flourishing and vibrant community. The members of the church were so kind, generous, and encouraging to us both, particularly in those early days.

We look forward to all that God will do in this city and beyond in the coming years.

Printed in Great Britain
by Amazon